Care Guide
Your Garden Pond

An Easy to follow Garden Pond Guide

Table of Contents

Introduction   3

Chapter 1: Your Garden Pond Needs You   5

Chapter 2: Caring for the Flora and Fauna in Your Garden Pond   10

Chapter 3: Cleaning Your Garden Pond Naturally   15

Chapter 4: Cleaning Your Garden Pond by Artificial Means   19

Chapter 5: Emptying the Garden Pond for Cleaning   21

Chapter 6: Common Myths   24

Conclusion   27

Introduction

Hello!

Garden ponds have the ability to mesmerize anyone and if you own one, I am sure you realize how fortunate you are. Water in any garden, park or a backyard seems to elevate the mood very few other things can. Everyone owning a garden, pool would want it to look sparkling clean and lively at all times. I am sure you too belong to this group. You too want your pond to look as beautiful and clean as ever.

You spent so much time, energy and money in creating your pond. You surely don't want all this to go waste. By creating a pond in your garden, you have initiated a self-sufficient ecosystem and you must do everything to sustain it. This book offers you simple and practical tips so as to enable you to keep your garden pond in top condition. When you care for your pond, it is easier to manage the flora and fauna that reside in it. You will see your pond flourish with a healthy population of fish, amphibians, plants and other wildlife.

Whatever type of pond you own – small or big, in-ground or above the ground or a simple pond or a landscape pond – all of them need maintenance and care. The size of your pond, the location and the seasons affecting it are some of the major factors you must consider while attending to it. You will find information related to all this and more in this book. Caring for your pond is the least you can do for the lovely fishes and plants that thrive in it. Nature plays its part in making your surroundings beautiful and peaceful. By regularly looking after your pond you are also reciprocating to the good things that nature offers you.

In this book, I have tried to share with you time-tested yet simple ways to take care of your pond. Once you read through the various chapters, you will marvel at how simple it is to effectively care for this beautiful water body in your garden.

It is time for you to become an expert at caring for your garden pond. One word of advice before we start – Remember to customize the guidelines shared as per your garden. No two gardens and their ponds are alike. The ideas and principles shared in this book take into consideration a wide variety of ponds. You know what is best for your pond. So use this book as a guide and do what you feel is best for your garden pond. So let's begin!

Chapter 1: Your Garden Pond Needs You

You have chosen this book so as to take better care of your garden pond, thus, I am assuming that you already have one with plants and fish in it. If the change in weather has resulted in your pond looking murky and like a pea soup, I guess it is high time you consider putting things on the right track. Let's look at some common issues you could face (or are probably facing currently) with your garden pond.

Common Issues
The basic thing you need to keep in mind while aspiring to own a healthy pond is clean and clear water with fit plants and fish in it. When you are able to do that, you will have a successful ecosystem booming in and around your garden pond. However, there might be some issues you may come across while trying to fulfill this purpose.

- **Persistent Water Loss:** There could be several factors responsible for the constant loss of water from your pond. Most of them are related to the building phase. You must attend to this immediately or your plants and fish will not be able to thrive for long.
    - Check the edges of the pond for leveling. When the pond liner shifts from its position there could be a loss of water leading to a drop in the water level.
    - Inspect the pond thoroughly by draining it completely. Transfer its dwellers into a container and keep it in the shade while

you take measures to arrest the leak. Hire an electric pump so as to expedite the process.
- Ponds having butyl liners could have gotten punctured. You can use a double-sided tape to address this.
- If your pond is made of fiberglass, it can crack if the ground under it is not leveled and consolidated in the right manner. If that is the case, purchase a fiberglass repair kit and let the compound solidify after you apply it on the cracks.
- A concrete pond leak is caused mainly because of the winter front. Examine the cracks and seal them with some mortar. Leave it for a day and then paint it with a water sealant.

- **Maintaining the Quality of Water:** This is very crucial for the health of your plants and fish. Good quality water is also safe from parasites and breeding mosquitoes.
  - Once you introduce fish and plants in your pond, make sure it remains clean and clear throughout. Pay attention to the health of the residents of your pond. If the number of fish goes down consistently, the first thing you must think of checking is the quality of water.
  - Keep a check on the algae. Algae steal the water of its oxygen, nutrients and salts, leaving very little for the other plants and the fish. Algae also grow into a dense layer on the surface, preventing sun rays from entering your pond.

Blanketweed is a type of algae that can choke your plants and restrict the movement of your fish. Get rid of them by pulling it out using a rake.
- Add oxygenating plants to your pond. They are efficient in absorbing the carbon dioxide in the water and also help in getting rid of algae.
- Get rid of dead leaves, broken stems and flowers. These decompose over a period of time and pollute the pond.

- **Issues related to Nature and Pests:**
    - Plants and animals compete amongst themselves for space, nutrients and water. This is natural. Pay attention to the plants in your pond. Every year, in late spring or during the onset of autumn, you must divide the overgrown ones. Divide the ones that have grown liberally and plant them in a different location.
    - Pests are quite uncommon when you have fish that feed on the insect larvae. However, in the summer, aphids might bother your water lilies and other plants. This can cause decay and discoloration of the leaves and flowers. Wash away aphids using a hose pipe.

- **Seasonal Issues:** Every season brings along with it some favorable things and some unwanted challenges for your garden pond. While this is true for all seasons, the autumn and winter seem to be the most awful ones in this respect.

- One of the most important chores in the autumn season is to keep dead leaves and the dry foliage away from your pond. This dying shrubbery decays and pollutes the pond, thus compromising the water quality. The best way to avoid this is to spread a net all over your pond. The smaller leaves and stems can be skimmed out using a pool net.
- The winter comes with its own bag of challenges.
    - For months your pond surface remains frozen and this traps in the poisonous methane gas that is produced because of the decay of the organic matter in the pond. This can be lethal to the fish.
    - If you have a concrete pool, the winter frost can cause the base of your pool to crack.
    - Try and keep your pool far from freezing by using a pool heater. This will keep one part of the pool surface open. You can also float a ball on the surface of the pond.
- **Predators:** Your fish could be attacked by predators like herons and cats. This is especially true during summer when the fish are swimming close to the surface of your pond for food, oxygen and sunlight. Provide a lot of cover for them during this season. Grow water lilies and lotus that can offer hiding spaces. You can also place rocks, clay pipes and small earthen pots under the water surface that can provide them shelter. Herons and cats can

really stress out your fish, so do address this issue. These were some basic issues that you can come across with your pond. Every challenge you face can be categorized into one of the above. It is important for you to recognize them before you go about maintaining your pond.

Chapter 2: Caring for the Flora and Fauna in Your Garden Pond

The fish and plants that live in your pond make your pond come to life. Without them your pond is merely a dead water body. Your pond is home to the flora and fauna living in it. Therefore, you must ensure that it is comfortable and clean at all times. This chapter mainly focuses on how you can care for these little dwellers of your pond.

7 Tips for Keeping Your Pond Fish Happy

In order to keep your fish happy and in the pink of health, you need to create a clean and favorable environment for them to thrive. The below mentioned tips will help you keep your fish and the pond in good condition.

1. **Install a Filter:** Keeping the water clean is a top priority. It is wise to invest in a good filtration system that will help in getting rid of the organic debris. Organic debris is not good for your pond as it will attract parasites and algae. Filtering plants like the Anacharis also help in keeping the pond naturally clean.

2. **Feed Fish Regularly:** Of course! Your fish need food. The fish in your pond definitely feed on the insects and plants in it; however, it is important that they get a balanced diet that is needed for their healthy living.
   - Invest in good quality fish food from a pet store

or an aquarium store. Talk to the shopkeeper about the type of fish you have and the kind of nutrition needed by them.
- If you are away for some reason, you can also procure a feeding station for your pond. This will keep distributing fish food at certain intervals in your absence

3. **Create a Shade for your Pond:** Your fish definitely need sunlight, but too much of it can cause sunburns and discoloration. Algae too love sun and multiply in the presence of sunlight. You should ensure your pond receives 60% of the sunlight at the warmest part of the day. You can do this by planting some bushes and trellises and vines near the pond.

4. **Clean Elements inside the Pond:** Frequently clean the rocks, tiles and ornamental elements (if any) in your pond. When you decide to change the water in the pond (do this at least once a month), scrub them with an algae scrub or hot water. Remember to rinse well before you re-introduce the fish. This helps in keeping the water clean and prevents algae blooms.

5. **Keep a Check on the Fish Population:** Too many fish in the pond can lead to lack of space, oxygen and nutrients. Keep in mind that your fish will grow and want to move around. You must make sure that the pond is large enough for them to breed. An overpopulated pond will generate more organic waste and is an open invitation for algae and parasites too.

6. **Clean off the Debris:** Your filter has its own limitations. It cannot get rid of the harmful debris like twigs, dead branches and other dead foliage. Moreover, you need to clean the filter and get rid of the muck that's stuck in it. You also need to keep a check on local insects and bugs that could feed on the food you provide for the pond fish.

7. **Drain the Pond:** The best way to keep the pond water fresh is to drain off at least 10% of the pond and refill it with clean and fresh water. This is the easiest way to clean your pond and maintain a healthy ecosystem.

7 Tips for a Healthy Flora

Plants are an integral part of your pond. Your fish will feed on it. Depending on the plants you choose, they also replenish the oxygen level in the pond. From multi-colored water lilies that float around your pond to aquatic forget-me-nots that cling the edges of your pond, you can count on all of them to add some color and life to your pond.

1. **Include a Wide Variety:** Aim for a good mix of plants – underwater, floating and emergent (the ones that grow out of the water). Randomly placing all sorts of plants in your pond will make it look interesting and will attract more wildlife.

2. **Experiment with Colors:** Colors attract everyone. Colors add liveliness to a landscape. Choosing lively colors – yellow, red, pink, orange and white – will make your garden

pond look like a paradise. Green foliage adds a sense of serenity to the surroundings. Include different shades of green and plant different textures in your pond.

3. **Know the Nature of Your Plants:** Before deciding on which plants you want to grow, you must know some basic things about them. Ask the gardener or the nursery owner about how big the plant will grow. The plant might appear small at first, but may grow large later. However, it should not take over the pond. Be sure to ask about their height and width. Also ask about the seasons they can flourish in. It is better to buy perennial plants that can keep your pond looking green throughout.

4. **Short first. Tall Later:** This comes across as a very basic tip. However, you must remember that the shorter plants are always at the front, while the taller ones take the back seat. This is the same principle followed while designing a landscape garden.

5. **Keep in Mind the Needs of Your Plants:** Keep in mind that your aquatic plants do not need a lot of sun. Too much sun can rob them of their color. Minimum 5-6 hours of full sun is required by your plants, but an excess of it and that too strong sunrays can adversely affect their growth.

6. **Not too Deep:** Aquatic plants should not be planted too deep in the pond. Plant them in the shallow area of your pond so that sunlight can reach them. This helps them flourish and this

provides for a variety of habitats. These were some basic tips that must be kept in mind while caring for the plants and fish in your pond.

Chapter 3: Cleaning Your Garden Pond Naturally

A pond beautifies your garden and its surroundings. Thus, keeping it clean is important, but can be challenging. Nowadays natural methods are used to clean the pond – barley straw and bio filters.

Step 1: Use a Biological Filter
A biological filter contains useful bacteria that help in getting rid of the organic debris. They are available as in-pond filters and external filters. You can choose from them.

- In-pond filters comprise of a pump that pulls water and this runs into a fountain. This is easy to install, however, it's not as easy to clean it. In order to clean it you will have to take the complete apparatus out.
- External filters are a bit easier to clean. Just one thing – you must check the size before purchasing it. It can be quite a challenge to find the right size for your pond as there are primarily for pools.
- The bacteria in the filter are not sufficient enough to take care of the toxins present in the entire pond.
- Buy a filter that has the capacity to filter twice the amount of water in your pond. If your pond holds around 2000 liters of water, you should consider buying a filter with a capacity of 4000 liters or more.
- The filter you buy should be able to

clean your pond within 2-3 hours. Definitely check the speed of the pump in your filter.

Step 2: Clean the Filter at Regular Intervals Most filters must be cleaned at least once a week. Cleaning is mostly simple. Just take a hose and use the pressure of water to get rid of the debris and muck stuck in the filter. Read the instructions mentioned in the brochure before cleaning the filter.

- Look for cracks in your filter. Pay attention to weird sounds or any leakage.
- If the filter you have has a gauge, be sure to clean it once the back-pressure crosses 4 pounds.
- Do not miss out on cleaning the filter. It can lead to your filter not working properly and will affect you and your pond adversely in the long run.

Step 3: Clean the Pond of Debris that the Filter Cannot
Your filter cannot do everything. Algae and dead foliage has to take care of by you manually. Use a garden rake or a long stick to get rid of any floating dead foliage. The only thing about manual cleaning is that you need to constantly keep a check for the floating debris and get rid of it instantly.

- Twigs, dry leaves, seeds, dry grass, flowers, and small branches can be easily taken out of the pond using a pool net. A special pool skimmer is also available for this purpose. You can

purchase this from a home care store in your area.
- Cleaning the bottom of the pond is also crucial. A pond vacuum cleaner or even a wet vacuum cleaner can serve this purpose. If you do not want to invest in one, you can also get it on rent. The pond vacuum cleaner will suck up all the debris that is lying at the bottom of the pond, thus cleaning the bed of the pond.

Step 4: Feeding Fish and Cleaning up We have already discussed about the how you must go about feeding the pond fish. Some things that you must bear in mind with respect to cleanliness of your pond –
- Choose a good quality fish food. Some cheaper options are available, but I would advise you not to use them as they do not get digested properly and also have the tendency to spread parasitic infections in the fish.
- Avoid overfeeding. You will get to know that you are overfeeding when you see bits of fish food floating on the surface of the water.
- The fish food you buy should be as per the type of fish you keep. Talk to an expert at the aquarium store about this.
- In winter and autumn, fish do not need a lot of food. The metabolism slows down during these months and hence you must reduce the amount of feed.

Step 5: Keep a Check on the Algae

Algae can take over your pond and rob the water of oxygen. Be sure to keep a constant check on it.

- Install a fountain or a waterfall. A moving water fixture will prevent algae and grime. The water will also be aerated regularly.
- Adding barley straw in the pond also helps. As it decomposes, it releases some chemicals that inhibit the growth of algae. 1 bale treats a pond of a capacity of 1000 gallons
- You can also use liquid barley. 2 tablespoons of liquid barley straw are sufficient to treat 100 gallons of water.

Chapter 4: Cleaning Your Garden Pond by Artificial Means

If you are not in favor of natural means or if you want quicker solutions, you can opt for chemical and mechanical ways of cleaning your garden pond. The chemicals and filters mentioned here are easily available at most gardening centers or aquarium shops.

Step 1: Use Chemical Treatment
A wide range of chemicals is available today to get rid of or inhibit the propagation of algae. These are also safe for your fish and the other wildlife that reside in your pond. Make sure you treat the water from time to time, especially when you see that the water has turned green.

Step 2: Use Gypsum
Gypsum (chemical name: calcium sulfate) is useful in breaking the sludge in the pond. Sprinkle it all over your pond surface at a concentration of 530 pounds/ acre-foot of water.

Step 3: Use an Ultraviolet Clarifier
These are a bit technical. UV filters pull water into a chamber where it is treated in the presence of the ultraviolet rays. These radiations kill the algae and other toxins. However, string algae are not affected by this treatment. UV light is harmful to the human eye and hence the bulb is encased in the UV

clarifier. While cleaning the filter, do not remove this case. A power of 8-10 watts works well for 1000 gallons of water. These UV filters can be attached to a mechanical or a biological filter and the clean water re-enters the pond.

Chapter 5: Emptying the Garden Pond for Cleaning

It is important to completely empty the pond once a while so as to clean it completely. Chemicals, filters and water treatment methods have their own limitations. They cannot address your problem completely and also cannot be overused. Thus, emptying the pond for cleaning becomes crucial.

Step 1: When Should You Consider Emptying the Pond?

If you find the water looking like a pea soup despite all the cleaning, it means that the bottom is still not clear of the organic debris. Dead leaves and sludge is still present at the bottom of the pond. This cannot be easily taken off by a pond vacuum cleaner and hence you must consider emptying the pond.

Consider emptying your pond and cleaning it at least twice a year. The best time to do this is during early spring before your fish start breeding or in the fall when you are making the pond ready for winter.

Step 2: Pump out the Water

You can either buy or rent out a pump for this cause. Usually, this pump comes with a long and an extendable hose pipe so that you reach the depth of the pond. Direct the water that is pumped out in your garden so as to avoid wasting water.

Step 3: Remove the Fish
After you have pumped out 3/4th of the water in the pond, start transferring the fish to clean containers with good quality water. This process takes time, so ensure that the water level is enough for the fish to swim and shallow enough for you to walk through.
- This is a messy process, so make sure you wear your rubber boots and gloves while doing so. The bottom is usually slippery, so use a support like a rod to walk around.
- Use a fish net to gently remove the fish out. A good quality and strong mesh will be required for all sizes of fishes so that they do not leap out. Step 4: Remove the Plants that aren't required Once you have removed the fish, it is now time to remove the aquatic plants from the pond. In case you have some useful plants, place them in a separate tank. Scoop out the dead plants and foliage.
- Use a pressure gun to spray out the sludge and to clean the bottom and the sides of the pond.
- Avoid using harsh chemicals and bleach that can make you regret later.
- Scrub out the base of the pond. Clean each and every tile and rock in the pond. In case you have some ornamental elements in the pond, clean them well by scrubbing them with an algae scrub.
- Remember to rinse the pond with clean water once you are done scrubbing the base. Step 5: Refilling Water in the Pond Once you are done with the cleaning of

the pond, it's now time to refill the pond with fresh and clean water. Add a dechlorinating agent to the water so as to get rid of the extra chlorine in the water. The extra chlorine can cause shock to your fish and plants and hence it is wise to follow this step before introducing the fish.
- When the pond is full to 1/4th of its total capacity, replace the plants and fish in the pond.
- You can buy dechlorinators from any aquarium store or a pet shop. Consult the store for advice on how much of this is needed for your pond.
- To make your fish feel comfortable with the new water and the environment, take a gallon of water from the clean pond and keep them in it for some time. After every hour slowly start introducing the fish in groups to the pond. Now you can refill the pond slowly to its full capacity.

Chapter 6: Common Myths

Today there is so much information available on a garden pond and its maintenance that you might wonder if all of it is true. This chapter will give you information of the common myths that exist in relation to a garden pond. You must be aware of these so that you do not feel overwhelmed by them.

#1 A Pond should be located at the lowest part of the garden. This is the worst location for your pond as everything from debris to the dirty water can flow towards your pond. This will make it difficult to maintain. A pond in and around your house is the best as it will add to the beauty of your garden and is easy to maintain.

#2 Ponds should be emptied and cleaned frequently. Over-filtering and over-cleaning can spoil the natural habitat. While it is important to clean the pond, doing it too often can disturb the flora and fauna. The fish and the plants in your pond feel unsettled and this can hamper their growth.

#3 You cannot be a Fish hobbyist and a gardener at the same time. This is definitely not true. In fact, both these can complement each other. Your fish will thrive on their own if you take care of the basics.

#4 Rocks and Gravel make cleaning tough. On the contrary, rocks and gravel provide plenty if hiding and breeding places for your fish. The aerobic bacteria in your pond breed in the crevices of the rocks.

#5 Predators are difficult and will eat up the fish. Raccoons and cats do not swim. The heron and the stork are potentially dangerous, but you can easily handle them by growing more of water lilies and lotus that offer plenty of shelter for your fish. You can also submerge earthen pots as these offer a good hiding spot for your fish. While planning your pond, you can also make crevices and small caves for them.

#6 Fish have to be kept indoors during winter. Fish are ok in the harshest of winters. Just ensure you have one very deep portion in the pond where they can hibernate. Use a pool de-icer that will keep a part of water from freezing. This will also allow the toxic gases to escape.

#7 A Pond brings mosquitoes along with it. Mosquitoes lay their eggs on the surface of stagnant water. Fish feed on larvae and hence there is no problem of mosquitoes because of the pond. Moreover, if you use a fountain or a waterfall, the water in the pond will not be stagnant enough for mosquitoes to lay eggs.

#8 A Pond cannot be located amidst a lot of trees. Yes, to some extent this is true as the dried leaves will pollute your pond. However, that can be taken care of by placing a net over the pond, especially during autumn. Your pond needs a mix of sun and shade. Too much sun can harm your fish and plants. So trees are great to have in and around the pond. Also imagine the landscape of your garden with trees and a water body. Priceless!

It is completely natural for you to feel overwhelmed by the huge load of information that is available today on maintaining your garden pond. However, before completely believing in it, you must evaluate it so that you are not under false impressions. This was the primary objective of this chapter.

Conclusion

I hope this book was able to help you to understand how you can effectively care for your garden pond. Having a garden pond is an asset and you are surely lucky if you have one. There a millions of people who long for a garden with a pond in it, and are unable to create one because of lack of space.

 Caring for your garden pond doesn't take much. I am sure by now you now have an answer for all the questions you had in mind about maintaining your pond. Now the next step is to effectively follow the practical guidelines shared in this book so as to keep this beautiful ecosystem in top condition. So go ahead and apply the tips shared in this book to effectively care for your garden pond.

Printed in Great Britain
by Amazon